There is not a single body in the grave

Debasish Tewari

There is not a single body in the grave

ISBN 978-93-5458-387-2
© Debasish Tewari 2021
Published in India 2021 by Pencil

A brand of
One Point Six Technologies Pvt. Ltd.
123, Building J2, Shram Seva Premises,
Wadala Truck Terminal, Wadala (E)
Mumbai 400037, Maharashtra, INDIA
E connect@thepencilapp.com
W www.thepencilapp.com

Author biography

Poet Debasish Tewari (short biography)

Born: 14th January 1982. He started writing poetry at a very young age. In 2002, he was introduced to the wider readership by publishing poems in the first Sharad Desh Magazine. Year Shardiya was invited to write in Anandabazar patrika. Profession: Teaching in government schools (Bangla language and literature).

So far, the number of books of poetry published by the poet is 9. The last book of poetry has been published by Ananda Publishers (Signet Press). He is also interested in translation literature. He has written many articles in the weekly Vartaman Patrika. Lots to love reading and walking.

CONTENTS

Cover design

Bhagirath Sardar

There is not a single body in the grave

.

I have translated the original Bengali poems into English.
I'm not very good at translating, but I'm just trying. The
translation of the poem may not have been as it is, but try
to write it down. I don't know how the readers will take it,
I have kept the original Bengali poems for the inquisitive
readers. Finally, I am grateful to the publisher for printing
the book.

Debasish Tewari
27/03/2021

Acknowledgement

My humble obeisance to my dear little aunt (Rita Pathak Tewari), the rare place and blessing I find after my little uncle.

1)

In the middle of the damp light wet yard in the afternoon
Your souls have fallen,
Those who have been neglected and neglected for many
years
Maya beside the remote bed
Was mediocre
Even then only two eyes in the light
He did not come out through the body
And today
Light in the afternoon
The death of their deaths, their spirits
There is no longer falling
Die.

2)

One day the winter guru
Inside A4 Cook, Table Booking Chak
Not blood, not meat - children, mud shaft - slopes
In the winter-winter match,
Tap-waters sitting straight, cold hands
Covering Herbos

                The night of the festival,

Night lightning
Profit!

3)

Mystery this time in the water-forest crowd
On the shores of the crowded fifties
Dancing suicide is fun, a light crack
Sometimes it is fun to spend the holidays
Delicious food will be sweetened with latex
The name behind the latex, who is running?
Playing in the floating distant forest
In the lap of the crowded fifty.

4)

Lots of water
The sound of fish fins can be heard
Swimming
Fish
Wants to stay in the dark
Dark look like
They are steadfast in light
Black of shaking
The water makes the waves
Fishers are unpaid, pauseous sounds
Is anyone hearing anymore?

5)

The two ways have covered the first snow
There are two waves in two ways
Going away from the road, moving away from the road
No one else can recognize!

6)

Who knows? Who says Mad?
Who understands Abol-Tabol
Only you can
To fry, a whole roll!

7)

On the day when the blood stream
On that day you showed a sadness
Standing to the neck of the evening
The lightning of the lamp.
Lamps did not burn, but smoke from flame ...
Some flowers flown,
Such a nidad
Did not take recognition and wrong.

8)

Know the name you called
Mixing the obsession of softness from side to side
Water rose from his softness
Lots of characters floated,
Somewhere in it is your nickname
And the consequences!
False food is floating in the writing
of water
I think it's straightforward
The way you call him
The way this amir will mix me
Whoever this is exaggerated
Surrounded
Not forever - he will go far
Deeper than any other time !

9)

Not Maya, the shadows turn and die
Back-to-back cavities
The idol that will come up from the chest of time is one
Remember Dhurjati !

10)

Ants have poison in their mouths
Aharnish said that he knew about this
Burn me?
But you know what?
There is no harm in not pouring poison
That's it
Peace-loving people, they think
Influence of time
Let the poison Aquarius drown
There is no harm
No harm done!

11)

Hand chopped chronic, handle towel slip
Ink
Otherwise
A-two vowels on the day of ad
Shrew the crowd
What will be the way? Now, what will be the way!

12)

This is a fresh life commotion, light
The black people are flat in the crowd ...
The population is black, tahe, black hair
Insufficient memory is mixing in the clouds
Memories are not insufficient, but abundant
From head to toe, commotion, marriage ...
Marriage is falling - a lot of light
Crowded in the crowd, the people are black ...

13)

Shyamalbarani marriage Kamalbarana
Sonaman is going flat, gold is going flat
Sonara is terrified, timid
Sonaman is flat ---- wake up decay!
Gold inside-out - afternoon light
Come evening, mother's name,
Ekadashi Palo.

14)

Sleep in this loneliness, fall asleep
Nazareth Church,
A little flame in it
How the plan will save the whole church
The old watch
Katchik Archiel is taking the money
He is also worshiped in the graveyard
Shubhra left after Armani Church
City is giving the church from afar!

15)

Away - the house of the breeze away
Can not handle,
Top like tough girls can not be scored
Whom the Japanese dolls say
That sat down, Iniesta, Messi

                              Tiara

Burma's Inner - Trophy Trophy
Throwing those
They are still not strong barbies, Japanese dolls
Away - the house of the breeze away
The goal is shouting and shouting flower!

16)

Sunshine
From Cherapunji on that way
If someone takes away a cloud
                    Oh, I'm angry!
Sleep-sleeping to Chile in Neon Light
                    And a little more today
How do you eat golden lunch?
War from the way,
                    The results do not judge
The way the cold air is tilt
That way goes more-once more
Why will go, he is next ...!

17)

There are a few polar sleeping in the night of the night
Away away - Relationships cause
Emperor Akbar after five minutes
He will go to the speaking person
War-alcohol
Clothes, throat tuning
I think - the emperor
But why he ...
Such a painful health, unbeliever, sympathetic
Flash waves
Why after hiring so much technicians
Rosi from the front of the eye
Do something from the earnings of all day
Carefully removed and filled her tin
Why this remake is in the door of the emperor
The second Akbar of 'Jodha Akbar'
Why are two eyes of the two eyes of the visitors
                    Emperor's souls?

18)

Shake the salwar kurta, shake the sun
Blaze
The desire to ignite that fire the night before
Storm of imagination
Keep pulling.
Pull-pull covers the fault
One or two layers of minerals
On a mat with fever,
Beneath the jumpsheet shed, she-ki flame glittered
Black on the outside, black on the inside
Four lights of decoration
Jumping and pulling
Blaze
Deliberately eighteen
Cutting thin shashi in the air
One or two useless sleeps in the dew
Keep moving,
I see him moving
He is flocking across our market
Millions
Thousands of birds,
One of them
With will
I hang it under the shed.

19)

They just wants to favor
Melts as far as to melt in heat
Team lighting with the context of having
Awaiting Duo

Rewards next to team pot. Body turn
The people are going to see. Lock lock
Fantasy income hanging with timeframe
The face is going to see these people who
Judgment!

20)

The way the fairies of the forest hide
The way Kandarpa-sahasi woke up in his mind
That's how you are with all the children today
You made a sharp sword

There was not the slightest affection in that Aussie
There was no other emotional pull
Was just daring
With the warrior-warrior attitude and this bone crush
You are depositing history in the abyss of time

The problem is the throat
Sometimes united
The dead marched and raised the flag
There is not a single body in the grave!

21)

Love talk to the flight fly-fly
The bird inside today is strange bondage
This understands the cage. This is another
Will kill the throat. The heart of the heart
The sound is broken. Syllable
Name wrote in the sand. Bali Bar
Leaving the temporary water
Fear of rejection! Love is in the bark
Fire of learning
Conducting bad so love-love
Washed in the water and the salary
The tongue leads to Swad, Love survived

22)

Light jacket in the fleet winter
See what the jet is flying in mind
Dress up
Before the coalition of the alliance replacement

Decoration, favorite jeans
Ideal trends missed ideal
Mistake-pan took after Frock
Waiting for color swelling ---- Hai!
What wait, dreamer
Scripture
Afterwards
In the counter color
As well as the monochrome mind cotton
Floats are in the bookpocket, laughing to come
He's smile
Do not be a couple
Masseling collar collar
Wrapping color, color
Men of the voice
Blue pink light yellow pendant
                    Dream dreams
Later
What do you want to bring? What do you want to bring

again
Aha-ray's mind floats the song
Before the escape of the escape
The fleeting afternoon is flying in the air!

23)

A-way
O-way
                Look at
Sleep broke morning and morning
Industrial
                Coming a khaki
For the love of her
Libids eat another
                Fear of fear
Like the leaves of the railway
As a result of abavation
                Appeared in the industry

24)

Revenge is falling on the cheeks.

Pieces of vengeance like aesthetics
Swallowing the gallbladder skeleton
If not, they will cross the border again
Build an old arena
And some names will be written in it

I told you the rhyme a long time ago

This time I said no or aesthetics

25)

Lanka-nun for gravy
What is the cheat in the mix of fivemisheli
One-two times the piston
Karat

From five-minute karat
The mind of the cup
Write food in fold
Distribution of Khandani

What is cooked - Beeli pulses
Sim-staff, cheeses
Write food inside the head
Spices Gizgiz

26)

Morning sleep looked at the breakdown
Delphi light
And shadows
Danger comes back
To this conscience

Chidakash wakes the song in the cloud
Rain sound
Or in the rhythm of a Gurujore Jumore
That song goes back
Any other dark

Heavy tree

27)

Everyone knows that way
The response to the name that called
Will say that, that name -
Any souls in the past
Recently, the shadow that did not go beside the name, her
Feeling insufficient
                    We've been avoiding
He is the fruit of the soul

I have moved away
Anyway in the east
                    Again ... again ...!

28)

The endless journey of style
Best wishes Priyadas Roy
Nehatai is the boss of desire, in the body of desire
The eyelids are flying, flying
Rustic dirty
Rustic dirty
One or two weak in the old style
The Maya of the word idol is corrupted
In the gap
Think of him
Endless journey of style, dimensional scene

29)

Tucal's pipe burst, water on the road
The reservoir is floating
Water is entering the paddy field from all around
Give this kindness, the heart wants the heart
However, the stream that the veins are carried out
The amount of losses when its side burst
    When the sudden proceeds come down
Keeping him in a vacant place .
Under the pipes of an angry pipe
Burning Rugs
    Copper fleshy paddy
This is the greeting -
What is the way to go?

30)

Women who dress now
The nudity broth falls
Older-Tradition in order

Currently gone to the height of the glamor
In the future, the girl may be in the future
It can also be New Born Trend,
Good-evil, after question
It also knows that the road goes bend
But, Krishna-day, that other
The words that write there
Who will blame in the nudity of this age?
Who guilty for clothes
That black age is today.
However, whose style
Hang our clothes today
Nudity is going to walk in sixteen trees.

31)

From Shimulgacha in the lice
Cotton flying
Cotton plaque, sprinkle
                    Head's hair,
Forget a little
Body cotton in the body
Sky kite
Shimul's branches were stuck in that
Do not know kites
But his fault
My forehead falling from the pulses
Then open the fate stopper,
Do you know what to do?
Will fly, and write,
                    Khan Khan rules!

32)

From drains to come to fresh foam
Opening the tucal's pipe.
Road
The footsteps of the gutgut gone far beyond
                    From the road to the field.
Then match-match
            Lying down and in the nearby village.
Not yet
Birds are like busy people at home
Sure comfortably
   Psychiatric sky songs
I see the light of light in the air
There is also glue in the glue!

33)

On the side of the road, there are cobras
Then the back path will be made
Where broken-broken
Khoya and sand are accumulating beside him
The long creek of Nyanjuli does not care about these
The water is empty,
So that more mosquitoes can accumulate,
Syringe-syringe blood will go to the mosquito's stomach!
The creek is widening the road
But the roads are dying.
In the light of night when he fell down exhausted without speaking
Passenger Zero,
A little more later the loud noise of the car
Pedestrians take away sleep!
A lump of stone falls
This is how this roadside game continues
Ten it was seen that that face is no more today
Just that
Under the mask
Some pedestrians walk in the night light!

34)

Purple color roar
Light and breeze
What is the pelestas of this cottage
            The coconut leaf above.

If dawn
Work correctness is my comfort
                Highlighting the little blinds.
Sleep
This is how to float in the pond
Fish, sell, spinach
Amani rice in two ways,
Spell in a small house in trients,
The sun is in the book
Selling someone's head
Comes and goes.
The doors are open to hats
Who will see?
                    That's like the busy room.
Someone is running in a tolerant, on top of two
All the family!
And
Tired farmers return home all day
This is dark
                Turn around the head.

Then make sure
Back home
Bossion
Arati rice
Breathing Falle in the Evening Evening,
As much as the soil, the soil, who laughs!
Who are talking around
                    Inside the light
In the voice of the ball
Who are walking around
                Ground
The bedroom
How many thoughts come, how many thoughts come
Beside him
This wounded erection
There is a bone river-canal-hill-mountain.

One-half day
Somewhat colorful
Seems somewhat gray
Inner fear
        As much as it leads to be small
In the light of the day.
Cyclopa
Run inside roast, then in the dark
                    The scandal is!

35)

By the side of the flyover
You look at the reservoir
You see Sonaman, you see the whole way
You see this eye.

The flyover flashed, burns in lantern light
Aleya's small-tiny life
Some people told
           Natural light of lack
The reservoir is sitting on the road, burning a whole day

You see Fools, some colorful!

36)

Boys in the game
A wide range of fields
The road in the grass, the row of bricks beside him
The sons of tomorrow are walking down tall legs.
The smiles of their faces have long been taken away,
As far as the light feels,
Actually it has been done in the society
                Sadly their childhood!

37)

Washing from the former-time
                    You and your mouth
The horizon is coming to the horizon
All doubt is crowding
                    Only in the head,
Then
Dry out of your two sides
I worn me
        The Maya-Maya reaches where darkness
You are also your o-face
Simply awake
                Do not miss!

38)

Morning news paper
The parallel is going out
Reading from news

                    Rood

Two words - rape, murder

What will happen from conscience away from the sun
What will reduce fire? (!)

39)

Beside the parashkol
A girl dropped down
I do not know the name, I do not know Dham - what's the
identity?
Its kinky to herb - Bahara!

Dipped on the neck of the towel
The girl's eyes,
I'm not, two friends again friends two sisters
Looking for a long time.

What is watching, just a bath - swimming swim
Dain from the bottom of the river!

40)

Mustard, not the mustard blossoms on the soles
of the feet
Shayasree has fled to the house
Even after that, whatever is there is Yashoda
Tarama fruit store
Who does these? Who eats them, who eats khaini fruits
The burden of justice
How to lose the head, how to lose?
In a way
Slipped away, the mustard yard moved
When judging the whole episode!

41)

Falls from
Winter bark
I'm sitting with pain
Keep in the lap
Filling a little bit of winter
This dawn has awakened with touch.

What is the dawn
                    Punja-Punja Nilima-Fennel
Detty!

42)

Dense fresh rudder
Fried is in the far sky
A little bit of the sky
Rudget Rudh
Adar-pitcher

Rudura
Eating is in the far sky
Varue to dense fresh flavor
Flown in the air-in-air

Air light
Oh, the hot grip!

43)

Celebrate the figures
My kids are going to bend today in the way of the apartment.
I say
That's just ten years old.
Why is it understood so much
Have you taken over?
They did not understand anything
Straight, in front of me.
Star-Star Memonic Kilobil-to-do
A number of people reaching.

44)

Age is like an icy chakravarti fascination
Comes straight, goes straight, extinguishes the eyes
What is the ceremony on the back of the circle?
We are all the people who step on it!

Loose-fitting food, sand, tends to get hot
People say Manglikai - gaps like opportunity
The work gets better, the work goes straight
Loose food, eats hot in the sand!

45)

The whole saddle has drowned her head
The neck line line, be clear-to
Then Balipoth is crossing
The opera of the empty path.

The way the gentleman does the king
But do not understand. The way the blind people
One part rush to be empty in any other way,
I am a poor Siraj Gonsai
According to a Tantra.

46)

Giving the higher secondary duty
Five students are sitting. The night did not sleep at night
They are students of science.
The waves came and gave tea.
Suddenly Abbas said, "What kind of things are you?"
Someone in my student-nobody
He is also afraid
                    There is no movement
One side of the chair was sitting in a direction.
Bamboo in the opinion of the window. She also kept
My duty is to fly into pieces-piece birds.

47)

The winter amazing hangs from closed corridor
The light of the light rowdy has become shared
The house of the house in Bengal.
Those who are hungry
Everyone's dietary rods
Has been severed.
Cleverness of satisfaction is no longer today
In the house of the world
Hanging, Rakabi amaz,
The trap of those who are in winter air.

48)

Clouds are stubborn clouds, rudder breeze
The blood is flowing.
Walk carefully today
Reached Bilaspur.
There are blood stains on the clothes
As many blood vessels
What is becoming colorful intoxication?
Life expectancy from the middle,
Falling in the mouth only kil
Do not pick up a beautiful woman open the door
Nightly sleeping fossil!

49)

I go to burn in the scorching sun
I have understood the whole being
Like bubbles thrown into the ocean floor of the world
In a simple heart,
This movement is frightened by the recessionary market
The way to constantly alulayita
And took away my dreamy sleep
In the role of traveler
I walk endless fields-forests-hills-twilight
Beyond
Beyond this movement, far beyond the horizon
Where the filthy evenings burn,
Two or three flowers bloomed.
Today the world is full of violence - the market is full of
cosmetics
Washing with benzoin is incurable
My whole being roared
There is no decoration on his face to burn
This disgraceful but stable being
Is covered
In one of the stagnation of another stasis!

50)

The bird hiding in the guava stalks
In the gap of justice
Don't bother me
Get some sleep, sticky, faucet floor
Beyond
Beyond the darkness of the bamboo bushes
The sound is anagona - chirping.

Calmly call the bird
A bunch fell from his nails
The madness of Kadambakeshar
So that you spread.

51)

In the absence of any other order
The bar of prohibition fell
He is busy
I see in aimless agitation.

His empty seat after flying in the air
Touching the ground
Pervasive
The way germs circulate in the blood-circulation.

52)

There is no dirt today
Numbness all around, two skeletal hands
When where leaves
Come on and chased poison!

Uncertainty has taken today
Some blessings.

53)

Krishna or the rural shepherd plays the flute
All sorts of hiya are stunned by the weight of the melody
The song that the fisherman is listening to on the tree
The ears have rotted while listening to the war
On the trunk of the headdress, the sword shone brightly
Willingly sitting in the shade of flowers

Today we have to forget violence as much as we can
It is a symbol of peace - a wooden sword,
The wind is swaying, the wind is blowing - the mind wakes
up in a frenzy
Forgetting the war feels like a touch of fresh melody.

www.ingramcontent.com/pod-product-compliance
Lightning Source LLC
LaVergne TN
LVHW050422160726

843469LV00041B/1193

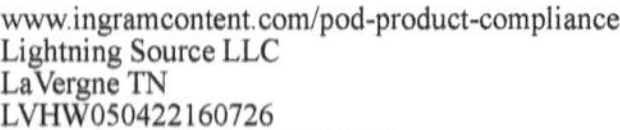